This copy of

SING A NEW SONG

comes to

....

with love from

....

Sing A New Song
Copyright © 1994 Eagle Publishing, Guildford, Surrey
GU1 4RF

British Library Cataloguing-in-Publication Data. A catalogue
record for this book is available from the British Library

Published in the USA by Harold Shaw Publishers, Box 567,
388 Gundersen Drive, Wheaton, IL 60189

Typeset by The Electronic Book Factory Ltd, Fife, Scotland.
Printed by L.E.G.O., Italy.

ISBN 0-87788-580-X

SING A NEW SONG

WELL LOVED HYMNS AND CHORUSES

Harold Shaw Publishers
Wheaton, Illinois

Whiter than snow

Lord Jesus, I long to be perfectly whole;
I want thee forever to live in my soul;
Break down every idol, cast out every foe:
Now wash me and I shall be whiter than snow.

Lord Jesus, look down from thy throne in the skies,
And help me to make a complete sacrifice;
I give up myself and whatever I know:
Now wash me and I shall be whiter than snow.

Lord Jesus, thou knowest I patiently wait;
Come now, and within me a new heart create;
To those who have sought thee, thou never
   saidst no:
Now wash me and I shall be whiter than snow.

James Nicholson

All things bright and beautiful

All things bright and beautiful,
   all creatures great and small,
All things wise and wonderful,
   the Lord God made them all.

Each little flow'r that opens,
   each little bird that sings,
He made their glowing colors,
   he made their tiny wings.

The purple-headed mountain,
   the river running by,
The sunset, and the morning
   that brightens up the sky.

He gave us eyes to see them,
   and lips that we might tell
How great is God Almighty,
   who has made all things well.

Cecil F. Alexander

Be Thou my vision

Be Thou my vision, O Lord of my heart;
Naught be all else to me, save that Thou art –
Thou my best thought, by day or by night,
Waking or sleeping, Thy presence my light.

Be Thou my Wisdom, Thou my true Word;
I ever with Thee, Thou with me, Lord;
Thou my great Father, I Thy true son;
Thou in me dwelling, and I with Thee one.

Riches I heed not, nor man's empty praise,
Thou mine inheritance, now and always.
Thou and Thou only, first in my heart,
High King of heaven, my treaure Thou art.

Ancient Irish tr by Mary Elizabeth Byrne
Versified by Eleanor Henrietta Hull

Great is Thy faithfulness

Great is Thy faithfulness, O God my Father,
There is no shadow of turning with Thee;
Thou changest not, Thy compassions they fail not,
As Thou hast been Thou forever wilt be.

  Great is Thy faithfulness!
  Great is Thy faithfulness!
  Morning by morning new mercies I see;
  All I have needed Thy hand hath provided,
  Great is Thy faithfulness, Lord, unto me!

Summer and winter, and springtime and harvest,
Sun, moon and stars in their courses above,
Join with all nature in manifold witness
To Thy great faithfulness, mercy and love.

Pardon for sin and a peace that endureth,
Thine own dear presence to cheer and to guide;
Strength for today and bright hope for tomorrow,
Blessings all mine, with ten thousand beside!

T.O. Chisholm
© Hope Publishing Co. 1951

I heard the voice of Jesus say

I heard the voice of Jesus say:
  Come unto Me and rest;
Lay down, thou weary one, lay down
  Thy head upon My breast!
I came to Jesus as I was,
  Weary, and worn, and sad;
I found in Him a resting place,
  And He has made me glad.

I heard the voice of Jesus say;
  Behold, I freely give
The living water; thirsty one,
  Stoop down and drink, and live!
I came to Jesus and I drank
  Of that life-giving stream;
My thirst was quenched, my soul revived,
  And now I live in Him.

Horatius Bonar
Permission of Oxford University Press

Be still, my soul

Be still, my soul: the Lord is on your side;
Bear patiently the cross of grief or pain;
Leave to your God to order and provide;
In ev'ry change he faithful will remain.
Be still, my soul: your best, your heav'nly Friend
Through thorny ways leads to a joyful end.

Be still, my soul: your God will undertake
To guide the future as he has the past.
Your hope, your confidence let nothing shake;
All now mysterious shall be bright at last.
Be still, my soul: the waves and winds still know
His voice who ruled them while he dwelt below.

Be still, my soul: the hour is hast'ning on
When we shall be forever with the Lord,
When disappointment, grief, and fear are gone,
Sorrow forgot, love's purest joys restored.
Be still, my soul: when change and tears
    are past
All safe and blessed we shall meet at last.

Katharina von Schlegel

Like a river glorious

Like a river glorious is God's perfect peace,
Over all victorious, in its bright increase.
Perfect, yet it floweth fuller every day;
Perfect, yet it groweth deeper all the way.

Stayed upon Jehovah, hearts are fully blest;
Finding, as He promised, perfect peace and rest.

Hidden in the hollow of His blessed hand,
Never foe can follow, never traitor stand;
Not a surge of worry, not a shade of care,
Not a blast of hurry touch the Spirit there.

Frances R Havergal
© Marshall Morgan and Scott

He leadeth me! O blessed tho't!

He leadeth me! O blessed tho't!
O words with heav'nly comfort fraught!
Whate'er I do, where'er I be,
Still 'tis God's hand that leadeth me!

He leadeth me, he leadeth me,
By his own hand he leadeth me.
His faithful follower I would be,
For by his hand he leadeth me.

And when my task on earth is done,
When by thy grace, the vict'ry's won,
E'en death's cold wave I will not flee,
Since God thro' Jordan leadeth me!

Joseph H. Gilmore

It is well with my soul

When peace like a river attendeth my way,
When sorrows like sea billows roll;
Whatever my lot, thou hast taught me to say,
"It is well, it is well with my soul."

Though Satan should buffet, though trials
   should come,
Let this blest assurance control,
That Christ has regarded my helpless estate,
And has shed his own blood for my soul.

O Lord, haste the day when my faith
   shall be sight,
The clouds be rolled back as a scroll,
The trump shall resound and the Lord
   shall descend,
"Even so"—it is well with my soul.

Horatio G. Spafford

Abide with me

Abide with me; fast falls the eventide;
The darkness deepens; Lord, with me abide
When other helpers fail, and comforts flee,
Help of the helpless, O abide with me.

Swift to its close ebbs out life's little day;
Earth's joys grow dim, its glories pass away;
Change and decay in all around I see:
O Thou who changest not, abide with me!

I need Thy presence every passing hour;
What but Thy grace can foil the tempter's power?
Who like Thyself my guide and stay can be?
Through cloud and sunshine, O abide with me.

Henry Francis Lyte (1793–1847)

O love that wilt not let me go

O love that wilt not let me go,
I rest my weary soul in thee:
I give thee back the life I owe,
That in thine ocean depths its flow
May richer, fuller be.

O light that followest all my way,
I yield my flickering torch to thee:
My heart restores its borrowed ray,
That in thy sunshine's blaze its day
May brighter, fairer be.

O joy that seekest me through pain,
I cannot close my heart to thee:
I trace the rainbow through the rain,
And feel the promise is not vain,
That morn shall tearless be.

George Matheson

Jesus, lover of my soul

Jesus, lover of my soul,
Let me to thy bosom fly,
While the nearer waters roll,
While the tempest still is high.
Hide me, O my Savior, hide,
Till the storm of life is past.
Safe into the haven guide,
O receive my soul at last!

Plenteous grace with thee is found,
Grace to cover all my sin.
Let the healing streams abound;
Make and keep me pure within.
Thou of life the fountain art,
Freely let me take of thee.
Spring thou up within my heart,
Rise to all eternity.

Charles Wesley

In Heavenly Love Abiding

In heavenly love abiding,
No change my heart shall fear;
And safe is such confiding,
For nothing changes here:
The storm may roar without me,
My heart may low be laid;
But God is round about me,
And can I be dismayed?

Green pastures are before me,
Which yet I have not seen;
Bright skies will soon be o'er me,
Where darkest clouds have been;
My hope I cannot measure,
My path to life is free;
My Saviour has my treasure,
And He will walk with me.

Anna L Waring

O God, our help in ages past

O God, our help in ages past,
Our hope for years to come,
Our shelter from the stormy blast,
And our eternal home!

Under the shadow of thy throne
Still may we dwell secure;
Sufficient is thine arm alone,
And our defense is sure.

Before the hills in order stood,
Or earth received her frame,
From everlasting thou art God,
To endless years the same.

O God, our help in ages past,
Our hope for years to come,
Be thou our guide while life shall last,
And our eternal home!

Isaac Watts

Photographic credits

Cover   Mackay, Thomas W, (1840–1916); *At the brook* (courtesy John Spink Fine Watercolours, London, © Bridgemen Art Library)

Page 5   Abels, Jacobus Theodorus (1803–1866); *A winter landscape* (courtesy Owen Edgar)

Page 7   Banks, William (1877–?); *Deer crossing a burn*

Page 8   Rigolot, Albert Gabriel (1862–1932); *A summer's day on the river* (courtesy Anthony Mitchell Fine Paintings, Nottingham)

Page 11   Strachan, Arthur Claude (1865–1954); *A beautiful herbacious border* (courtesy Haynes Fine Art, Broadway, Worcs.)

Page 13   Mackay, Thomas W, (1840–1916); *At the brook* (© Bridgeman Art Library)

Page 15   Darien, Henri-Gaston (1864–1926); *Une chaumière et un coeur* (courtesy Galerie Berko)

Page 16   Monsted, Peder Monk (1859–1941); *A shady stream* (courtesy Burlington Paintings, London W1)

Page 19   Shalders, George (1825–1873); *A shepherd boy and flock of sheep* (© Bridgeman Art Library, courtesy Christopher Wood Gallery, London)

Page 21   James, David (active 1883–1897); *The flowing tide* (private collection)

Page 23   Cole, Reginald Rex Vicat (1870–1940); *September leaves* (courtesy Nick Drummond)

Page 25   Lundby, Anders Andersen (1840–1923); *The woods in silver and gold* (courtesy Polak Gallery, London SW1)

Page 27   Monsted, Peder Monk (1859–1941); *The lake in the woods* (courtesy Burlington Paintings, London W1)

Page 29   Mitchell, C L (circa 1900); *A day at the river* (courtesy Anthony Mitchell Fine Paintings, Nottingham)

Page 31   Knowles, George Sheridan (1863–1931); *The rose arch* (courtesy Walker Gallery, Harrogate)